D1460170

www.visiononpublishing.com

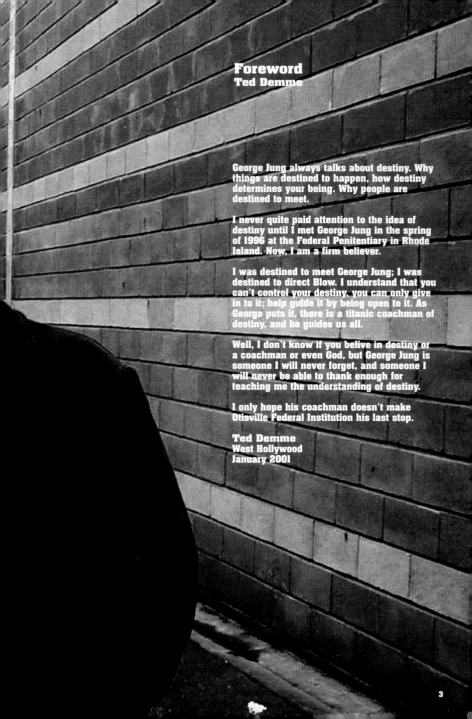

Foreword
Ted Demme

George Jung always talks about destiny. Why
things are destined to happen, how destiny
determines your being. Why people are
destined to meet.

I never quite paid attention to the idea of
destiny until I met George Jung in the spring
of 1996 at the Federal Penitentiary in Rhode
Island. Now, I am a firm believer.

I was destined to meet George Jung; I was
destined to direct Blow. I understand that you
can't control your destiny, you can only give
in to it; help guide it by being open to it. As
George puts it, there is a titanic coachman of
destiny, and he guides us all.

Well, I don't know if you belive in destiny or
a coachman or even God, but George Jung is
someone I will never forget, and someone I
will never be able to thank enough for
teaching me the understanding of destiny.

I only hope his coachman doesn't make
Otisville Federal Institution his last stop.

Ted Demme
West Hollywood
January 2001

PLEASE KEEP
AREA CLEAN
POR FAVOR
CONSERVE
LA LIMPIEZA

Director
TED DEMME

George Jung

Ted Demme Breaks into Jail

Interior Cell Block – Day

Cop You've got a visitor, George.

George Who is it?

Cop Guy named Demme – looks important, drove up in a limo wearing a baseball cap – says he wants to put you in the movies.

George Did he bring Camel Straights?

Cop Two packs.

George Tell him I'm on my way.

Interior Visiting Room – Day

Ted George, I'm Ted Demme and this is Nick Cassavetes. We represent Spanky Pictures and Darn Good Films.

George (V.O.) Shit! A kid in a baseball cap and a seven foot guy with tattoos – what the hell is this? Where's Louis B Mayer?

Spanky Pictures, 'Spanky and our Gang', right?

Ted Right on, George, and Nick here makes Darn Good Films.

George Good Christ! In the end it all comes down to this.

Nick Don't get uptight, man – we had to break the bar code to get in this joint.

George Fuck the bar code to get in, what's the code to get out?

Ted Easy, everybody knows that.

George EASY! What the hell is it, man?

Nick Cool it man! You look like a smart guy. I mean you made a dump truck full of money.

George Just give me the code – everybody keeps talkin' about the money.

Ted Easy, George – the bar code is 'God equals one, Satan zero'.

George That's it! Sure it's not the other way around?

Ted Nope – that's it.

George Satan zero, no points – I'm fucked! Never getting out of here, what the hell, at least I rolled up the last page of *On the Road* and smoked it. Maybe Tuna had it right when he walked off into the Mexican sun lookin' through his head for Neal Cassady – he traded in his peace sign for Pancho Villa's horse, you know. After that, Timothy

Leary dropped out thinkin' he was in while Dylan was pissed off somebody let Albert in the hall. You know I never really became old – I was just fuckin' tired of time.

Ted I was thinking – how were you able to live without falsehoods?

George When you live outside the law you must be honest.

Nick Dylan, right?

George (V.O.) Well shit. Maybe this guy with the tattoos can get a screenplay together. It's got to be a bitter sweet novella without sanctuary.

Ted Exactly my thoughts, George – something like, there is no God but reality and you are a true sky pilot going down blinding unfrequented paths where every taboo is Holy.

George (V.O.) Man! I like this kid in the baseball cap – OK, Spanky, let's roll. OK, Teddy bear, riddle me this;

what if the dream came true? Is there really a medicine man? Were the black hats really white? Is there a paradise without a home? Does every paradise have a serpent? Will time's passage reveal the truth of it all? Will you tell them of my dream and sing a song that is so merry? Will you tell them of my loves, 'O so sad'? In the end, will they know that the Gods surely made me mad?

Ted All this and more, my boy. What I'm looking for is an ounce of psychological credibility to help them identify with your unscrupulous ambitions. It will be really the ultimate in mayhem cartoons about an annoyingly garish Jesus Christ Superstar – You!!

A guy with fast pace, corrupt in a Columbian Renaissance court with no dress code – you pretend to be virtuous, cruel and lustful while you deliver proclamations of innocence – you're an arrogant tauter with more corkscrew twists than a wino. Your

noble soul is contaminated when you meet your Queen at a Cotillion Ball in Hell! She keeps a black book on criminal proceeds and constantly takes baths to cleanse her soul. It's really about your game, which is called No Ceiling. Those around you try to play without knowing the rules, which were made for the wise men and the fools.

George Go ahead, Ted – you tell it better than I think of it. Are you sure about the bar code? You know the Devil being zero and all. I mean, there are still a lot of timeless mysteries and many things left undone. Maybe I'm really lost and not even God can find me.

Blow
by
Blow

Based on the motion picture 'Blow' by New Line Cinema.

The making of the film with digital photography by director Ted Demme.

Words by Ted Demme and Johnny Depp with Poems by George Jung.

Selected dialogue from the screenplay by Nick Cassavetes and David McKenna.

Introduction
Johnny Depp

I arrived in New York City late, somewhere around 11.30pm, from Europe. With just enough jet lag to keep my peepers wide open for one too many hours – my brain crowded with the threat of Mr Sun's arrival, knowing that soon he'd nudge me out of my snooze and into the world. I shut my eyes tight with the hope that he might be tardy.

Woke up the following morning – or rather, a couple of hours later – with a very prompt Mr Sun stabbing through the black protection of my eyelids. The rotten bastard had found me.

I pitched and tossed and turned and spun – doing my best to avoid him – until I just couldn't take it anymore. I forced the heavy lids up and open and stared the eyeballs straight into the beastly light. I dunked my face into the pot of hot coffee and dove out the window and thus began the day. Things to do… Up. Awake. Onward. Forward.

I made my way downtown to St Mark's Place to a bookstore of the low-down, the lowbrow, the bohemian, the subterranean-counterculture-drop-out types. My mission – to get my paws on some fine literature suitable for… well, you'll find out. First and foremost, *Fear and Loathing in Las Vegas* by the

good doctor himself, Dr Hunter S Thompson – a must for anyone and everyone… especially anyone in need of a serious excursion from their four walls. Second on the list, *Tarantula* by Bob Dylan – we need say nothing about him or his genius. Third, Kerouac – anything at all by ol'Jack… *On The Road* being the Bible. And why not throw in a little taste of Burroughs and Ginsberg while I'm at it.

I was taking these fine books to prison, to Otisville Federal Correctional Institution, to be specific. I was to meet up with one George Jung, a guest of said facility, Federal Inmate #19225-004.

The ride upstate took a coupla' few hours – I used this time to get through the several thousand questions that swirled inside my head, destined to be received by Mr Jung. I pondered the answers and then threw them out of the window as I arrived at the prison.

A thick comfort of snow lay on the ground – the sun still pointed in my direction – I found myself standing outside the fence of a bland-looking institution with the benign façade of any Department of Motor Vehicles. And that's exactly what the place felt like inside… that is, until the first

set of steel doors. Loaded down with many packets of filterless Camels for Federal Inmate #19225-004, the books purchased on my earlier mission and a pocketful of change for the soda pop machine (one of the very few luxuries allowed at visiting time), I was taken through the congested maze of inmates and their wives, children, lawyers and guards to a small room surrounded by reinforced glass, more steel doors, more buzzing, more clanging, etc. Within a minute or two of waiting in my fishbowl I was introduced to Inmate #19225-004. He stepped up with a crooked half-smile, deep squinted eyes and the weathered, broken, damaged soul of a pirate who'd seen too many days at sea. We greeted each other casually, if a bit warily, and within three minutes – and from then on, he was George and it was as if we'd known each other for a thousand years… or more.

For the next several hours we talked intensely… him doing most of it. I listened and watched him like a hawk. Spewing tale after tale, esoteric analogies, fact after fact, each one topping the previous. He was generous, he was gentle, he was hilarious, he was heartbreaking, he was all too human – a kind of outcast Zen Master who'd grabbed hold of

life by the short and curlies and swung it around for all it was worth. Life, then, snuck up on him and bit him hard on the ass.

Among the many amazing wisdoms that George so generously shared with me, there is one in particular that haunts my thoughts constantly: 'One is the number and two is the one'. The most frightening thought of all is that I'm pretty sure I know what he means.

It's very rare in life that any person opens up their heart and soul to you with unlimited access to their most profound thoughts, dreams, fears, regrets, intimacies... even more rare when you've just met that person and, because of the obvious predicament, it's highly unlikely that you will be spending too much time with them in the near future. So for this and more, I owe a great debt of gratitude to George. And also for the honour of meeting him, knowing him, learning him and learning from him. All of this, along with the opportunity to portray George, was made possible courtesy of Ted Demme and Nick Cassavetes, who were the guys who had the nuts to take the ball and run with it in the first place.

I was asked to write an introduction to a book – a book that I know nothing about.

They tell me it's a book of photographs and that these photographs were taken on the set of *Blow*. I don't know how to write about that. What I do know is, anything that happened on the set of that film only happened because of George... so I wrote about him. And although he was the one major ingredient that was physically missing from our set, his strength, his energy and his spirit was omnipresent.

To the Federal Government, George Jung is nothing more that a whooper stack of papers shoved into a filing cabinet collecting dust, another notch on their belt.

To Otisville Federal Correctional Institute, he is merely Inmate #19225-004.

To his daughter Kristina, he is the father that she was never given the possibility of knowing or loving.

To me, he is not a number, he's not a convict, and he's not a criminal. He's a great man whose wisdom and knowledge, unfortunately, was greatly overshadowed by the choices and mistakes he made all those years ago when he hadn't even had time to brush himself off from the conditioning wrought upon him by his parents.

As I write these words and as you read them, George is almost definitely sitting on his bunk in a 4 x 8 foot cell, dreaming of the day that he, too, can be standing outside the fence of that bland-looking institution, far away from the clanging, buzzing steel doors of the inside...a thick comfort of snow on the ground, the sun pointed in his direction...Up. Awake. Onward. Forward.

May the wind always be at your back
And the sun upon your face
And the wings of destiny to carry you aloft
To dance with the stars...

Johnny Depp
France
Friday 13 April, 2001

George Jung
JOHNNY DEPP

Some kind of happiness
George Jung

"While considering your options, remember this and remember it well: choice without consequence is no choice at all."

I'd like a word with the producer. I demand to star in this humungous giant spectacle called 'My Life'. I can and will star in the movie – what the fuck; everybody's performing, we only think it's real. One has to have a passion for this insane occupation. It's like a relationship, which occasionally fulfils a person, but only a collision can transform him.

You must have the passion. Passion, you must understand, isn't a path through the woods. Passion is the woods! Passion is your mistress and you are driving to open her legs like a free checking account at the Bank of America.

You're intoxicated knowing you're not starring in the movie. You are the Movie! Coming into Los Angeles. Bring in a couple of keys.

You're the Salvador Dali of nose candy. You're the Day-Glo Christ. You're the Quick Silver messenger service. You intensify the solar palette. You fuel the dragon's fire that sleeps in ancient vapours while the teeth on the totem pole chatter.

"ARE WE GOOD? YEAH, WE'RE GOOD. WE'RE BEAUTIFUL, WE'RE PERFECT. THIS IS ONE

HUNDRED
PERCENT PURE
COLUMBIAN
COCAINE,
LADIES AND
GENTLEMEN.
DISCO SHIT...

...PURE AS THE

DRIVEN SNOW."

Ermine Jung
RACHEL GRIFFITHS

"I was sitting there, and it was like the outside of me and the inside of me didn't match, you know? And then I looked around the room and it hit me. I saw my whole life. Where I was gonna live, what type of car I'd drive, who my neighbours would be. I saw it all and I didn't want it.

Not that life."

Young George Jung
JESSE JAMES

Fred Jung
RAY LIOTTA

Young Tuna
ALAN JAMES MORGAN

George Jung Are we gonna be poor?
Because I don't ever want to be poor.

Fred Jung Look son, this is the way it goes.
Sometimes you're flush. Sometimes you're
bust. When you're up, it's never as good as it
seems. And when you're down, you never
think you'll be up again.
Life goes on.
Remember that.
Money isn't real.
It doesn't matter.
It just seems like it does.

George No, Dad.
I don't want to... I mean, I just don't want...

Fred You don't want to be like me.

George No, Dad. I don't.

Fred What are you going to do?

"I'm going to California."

A Best Friend
George Jung

If God is really of no specific gender, this I do know: as a child I found God in the form of a man who was my father. I loved him then as I do now, though he is now but a shadow of my imagination. Early memory going back over a half century. Pulling on his pant leg, he'd leave for work leaving me in a fit of rage and disappointment, rushing to the window he'd disappear into the morning sun. It was all a mystery only knowing when darkness came upon the world he'd return.

I know the sound of his footsteps along with the beats of my heart. He was a giant lifting me high repeating, 'It's okay son, I'm home.' Tears welled in his eyes, which took me a lifetime to understand. We were one but as two beings consumed by a love equal to the intensity of the sun. It was God at the height of his perfection. One was the number and two was the one. A man and his son. Time wore on allowing the choice between folly and sacrament, and the existence of the world begun to pull at the sacred golden thread which held us so close. This man became familiar to me and I no longer waited fearing he'd not return. He was being replaced by my own individuality and my endeavour in folly. However, out of respect for him, I placed him into my miniature world of toys in the form of a truck exactly like his giant one.

This pleased him no end. It was all very simple as long as he was happy. There were, however, brief interludes when he was sad, causing me to be sad as if we were of one heart. Why this great man existed was all a wonderment to me which I dared not question for fear he'd disappear. There were other giants in the kingdom, but mine, of course, was the best one. This was never refuted and still isn't. However, in every perfect union there are flaws. Freedom began to echo which consumed my being causing me to test the Giant's will. Sometimes it was all too easy.

The Giant would give in to me with laughter, causing me great confusion along with a feeling of pride. In the course of time we became equal in size, although never in wisdom. He would watch my victories and defeats over the years with keen interest, waiting patiently for the exact time he deemed necessary to offer bits of wisdom and caution. For the longest time he just seemed to be one of the many parts of my life. I'd grown into adulthood and was consumed with the self. When he became an old man, it's true I would sometimes forget about him for long periods of time. Forget about the multitude of gifts he'd given me, all precious beyond gold. I got lost along the way and began to look for the old man and found him down an unfrequented path which led to my heart.

Now, I stand inside his shoes and he in mine. His voice echoes within my being, a song of love, and together we throw horseshoes at the moon. Knowing you can't be a loser if you never lose your pride, we laugh and stay forever young chasing the wind, knowing the good times were pure as diamonds.

CALIF

ORNIA

WEEKLY
SPECIAL

COFFEE
SHOP

Tuna
ETHAN SUPLEE

George California was nothing like
I'd ever experienced.

The people were liberated and
independent and full of new ideas.
They used words like 'right on',
'groovy' and 'solid'.

The women were all beautiful and
seemed to share the same
occupation…

Barbara
FRANKA POTENTE

Maria
MONET MAZUR

Barbara "...I'm a flight attendant."

"I don't know about you, but I think we're gonna like it here."

29

"We want some grass."

Derek Foreal
PAUL REUBENS

George What the fuck is that?

Derek It's your grass?

George Wow! That's more than we had in mind.

Derek I don't nickel and dime. You want it or not?

George We'll take it.

George This is it for me.

Barbara What is?

George Just everything. You. California. The beach.
This spot right here.

"I feel like I belong here, you know? It just feels right."

Tuna Well, look at what the cat dragged in.

George Holy shit, Dulli. What the hell are you doing here?

Kevin Dulli
MAX PERLICH

Franka
George Jung

Few people, very few indeed, are allowed the privilege of a rerun, at least not here on earth. You truly celebrated every aspect of a special lady with whom I lived in a realm of consciousness known only to lovers – that interplay of men and women in the engine that runs the universe fueled by the embroidered memories of lovers.

We searched and found a sanctuary where Heaven and Hell intermingled, as they did no other place on earth, except in the emotions of poor fools in love.

We lived alone together kissing each dawn upon her lips, while the wind cried. We danced a tango in a runaway sky surrounded by electric pink clouds entwined in each other's ancient vapours. Dense and penetrating the gap between nature and civilisations where forgotten longings stir the dragon's fire. Paradise is not lost, it sleeps in your ancient soul and I, the keeper of precious moments lost in time, walk in the wilderness too tired to make it home.

Dulli Do you know how much money I could make if I had this stuff back east?

George We need to get to the source...

"Who speaks Spanish?"

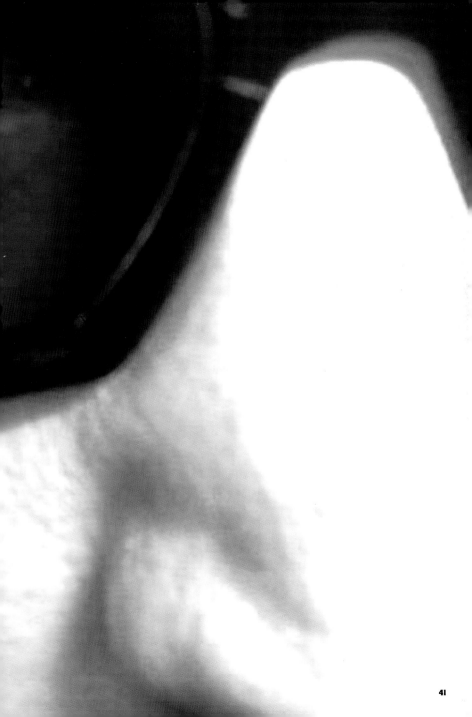

"Have you got any dope?"

"Ramon tells me you are looking for some mota?"

"I'll take all of it. I'll be back in a week with a plane."

"I can't believe we're stealing a plane."

"Don't be such a pussy. It's fine. We're not stealing it, we're borrowing it. And try to look natural."

"Good to see you, Jorge.

"You are a man of your word."

Barbara Surprise!

George Baby, you didn't have to come.

Barbara What, and miss all the fun? C'mon, not a chance. So, what's the verdict?

George Lawyer says he can plead it down to five years. I'll serve two.

Barbara Two years. George, I can't wait that long.

George What? You're not going to wait for me?

Barbara George, I went to the doctor. I don't have two years.

"Which brings me to rule number three, which says, fuck rules one and two, skip bail, and take off."

Fred I just don't understand what you're thinking. I don't understand your choices. You know, the police are looking for you.

George I know. I'm great at what I do, Dad. I mean, I'm really great.

Fred Let me tell you something, son. You would have been great at anything.

"So, go to jail. It's for your own good. You need to straighten your life out."

Diego Delgado
JORDI MOLLA

"Don't worry. We'll talk of everything. We have the time. You arrive here with a Bachelor of Marijuana, but you will leave with a Doctorate of Cocaine."

"Allo?"

"Diego? It's George."

"George, hello! Today is the day, eh? Are you out?"

"Yeah, I'm out."

"Congratulations, my brother. I've been waiting for you."

"How are you doing?"

"Perfect, George. Perfect. Everything is fine down here. Everything is all set up."

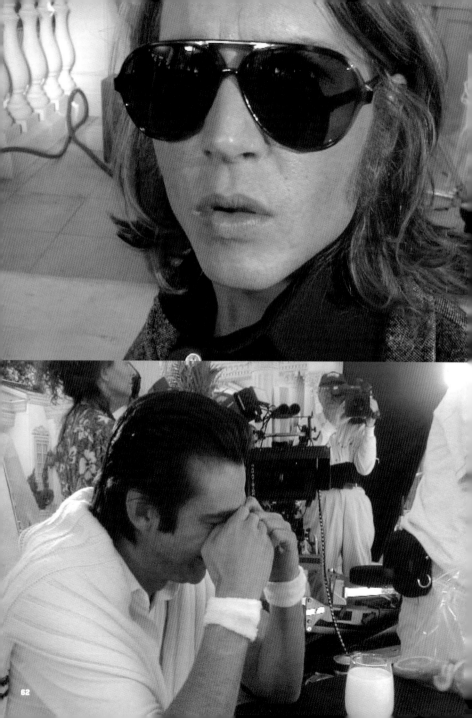

Cesar Not so fast. I would like to go over the details.

George What details? I put the coke in the false bottoms and take it through customs.

Cesar Tell me about the suitcases. What is the make and the colour?

George Samsonites. Red. No tags.

Cesar Hmmm. I see. Will there be clothes in the suitcase?

George What? Yeah, sure.

Cesar Whose clothes? Your clothes?

George My clothes, your clothes. What does it matter?

Cesar I would like to know the contents. Every detail is important.

George What are you doing here, Diego? This guy's a clown. He's talking about clothes.

Cesar I demand to know everything. I do not trust six hundred thousand dollars of coca to someone I don't know.

George It's a lousy fifteen kilos. I piss fifteen kilos.

Cesar The coca is my responsibility!

George You're a fucking amateur!

Diego Gentleman, please. There is no need to be impolite. Cesar, this will be fine. You have my word. George, Cesar is just being thorough, that's all.

Cesar Very well. But just remember, Mr Jung, I will be with you the whole way, and I will be watching.

"When you're carrying drugs across the border, the idea is to remain calm. The way I do it is to think of something pleasant, a fun party, a moment of triumph, a sexual encounter. I actually project myself to that place. Anything to keep your mind off the fact that you're going to jail for a very long time if they find fifteen kilos of cocaine in your suitcase."

"What we're doing is measuring the purity"

Mr T
BOB GOLDTHWAIT

George There was an 85% chance that if you snorted cocaine between 1977 and 1984 it was ours. Initially, with my LA connections, we invented the marketplace. In 1977 there was no other real competition. The first year we made $100 million between us. It was an expensive operation. Eventually we built up to three different pilots doing multiple runs per week, connections on both coasts: everything was running smoothly.

"We were like a corporation."

Derek It's great and everything, but what am I going to do with all of this?

George Sell it?

Derek Jesus Christ, George, I don't see you in two years, and you show up at my door with a hundred and ten pounds of cocaine?

George Just sell it, Derek.

"All right, but it's gonna take me a year..."

Derek ...Thirty-six hours. I can't believe it. Everything gone in thirty-six hours.

George I think it's fair to say you underestimated the market there, Derek.

Derek Touché.

George But to the victor belong the spoils. Half a million for you. Half a million for me. One point three five for the Colombians.

Derek Nice doing business with you, George.

"Not bad for

a weekend's work, huh?"

Pablo Escobar "The man who gives us the airplanes. The man from America. The Mafia. Chicago, boom, boom. Hollywood.

You are going to open the gates of Hollywood, George? So you are wanting to sell the cocaine for me, George?"

"With all respect, Padrino. Diego is my partner. I do not do business without him."

Lust

George Jung

The women I lusted for throughout my
sorted life had a biological drive all
right, only it wasn't for babies. It was
for cash. They longed to swell up with
a pregnancy of moola and expel silver
dollars like a slot machine. It was
always the same rendezvous on a bed
of weirdness, screwing slot machines
while their fingers dipped like rat fangs
into my wallet. They all seemed to
have exes who resembled Spanish
peanuts dancing demonically and were
as loose as a collar around the neck of
eternity running to catch the sunset.
You either simply evoke lust or you
struggle to dominate it, taking the
first bite and washing it down with
the wave. Don't get lost in Nirvana
asking the question, 'Where the hell
am I?' Lust traffics in illusion and
surrogate boredom; victims all waiting
for a ticket to Timbuktu where you
ride Mustang Sallys in multicoloured
caftans with purple turbans and
Buddha on perfumed acreage. It's
always more than likely a short ride
but it takes you where you want to
go, wherever the hell that is. Why
concern yourself with trivia? If you
unravel you can always re-ravel.

"I'm married, George."

Inez
JENNIFER GIMENEZ

"Me. I can't believe it."

Beneath a gunsmoke sky
George Jung

Virtue is not something you can win in
a goddamn lottery.

The Iguana Woman was a cross
between Bo-Peep and the wild thing
with a glimmer of primal Eve. She had
eyes like chocolate-dipped cherry
bombs with their fuses lit. Eyes so
fierce she could stare down John
Wayne and hypnotise Houdini.
Meeting her was what shitless folks
call luck. The wise ol' boys call it
Karma. Her virtue was wrapped up like
a pharanic Burrito which I, more than
ever, wanted an Aztec-sized bite of.

The Iguana Woman was more that a
mere cocktail of emotions to my heart
– she was castanets and silver whips.
She was the show-stopping white
pony. She was the connection to the
Toot Tree. We had it all: the Toot Tree,
the Airstrip; and I was going for it –
besides, the story doesn't know who's
telling it and minds were made for
blowing – I'd recently come through a
crisis of sorrow and betrayal inherent
in any endeavour led by the ambitious
and the bloodthirsty.

There are times we can feel our own
destiny close around us – sure we can
resist leaving the Gods to walk away in
disgust, depriving us of another chance
in life to swing open into unnecessary
risk and enchantment.

"I know who you are, El Americano. Mister George."

George I do.

Mirtha I need a fucking drink.

You better know what you're doing, George. You're playing with fire.

George I like fire.

Diego Three years. How
long have we been in
business? Three years?
Does she get to meet your
connection? Was she good
enough?...

George Shut up, Diego.
They're going to be here any minute.
I'm trying to concentrate...

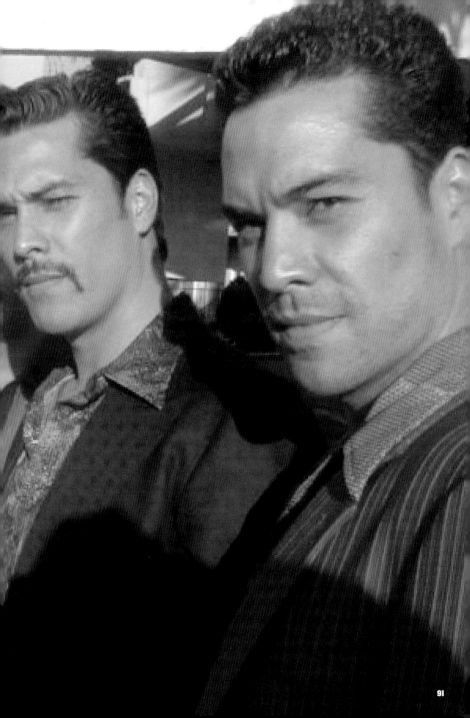

Diego I'm very angry with you, George. Very angry. You don't take me to California, but you take your bitch wife? A woman? I understand you love her, but it was you and me who started this. You and me.

George What do you need my connection for, Diego? What are you going to do with it?

Diego What do I do with it? Nothing. It's for peace of mind. It's for the principle.

George Jesus fucking Christ, Diego. I ain't telling you. It's just business. Now, shut up. You're driving me crazy.

"Derek Foreal. Derek fucking Foreal. All right? The answer to all your dreams. Are you happy now?"

"Hello, Derek? This is George.

Am I wearing lipstick?

I said, am I wearing lipstick?

Because when I'm getting fucked, I
want to make sure my face is pretty.
You're buying directly from Diego,
aren't you, you son of a bitch."

Greed
George Jung

An island in the sun. A place where only the wind and the wild men go. An island wherein lies a pool of reflection and the monster of reason. I myself, a fugitive madman in a waistcoat. My profession: a master of games. Are men not born of games? Nothing else. Every child knows games are more noble than work. He knows too that the worth or merit of the game is not inherent in the game itself but rather in the value of that which is put at hazard. Games of chance such as this require a wager in order to intensify their meaning.

The wager being life itself. I chose to play a thousand lifetimes ago and was still hard at it sitting at the table with pirates, cut-throats and master thieves, all my comrades and opponents. I did not come easy to this place in time. It was all by trial of worth and risk, having only your life to wager, where a wrong choice swallows up a game, player and all.

I ask you: what more validation of a man's worth could there be? Ah! The enchantment of the game. It is not a drug itself when played to its ultimate state and surely leaves no argument as to the winners and losers. To win is ultimate. The winner becomes a God driven by a torch whose brightness sets back the stars in their sockets.

What is the fate to be for? A player in the greed game? Let me tell you, friends, trust me in this for I know it to be true. I will not cheat you of such knowledge. It all comes to an end as games of course always do. When the others have gone and only the game is left with its solitary participant. A solitary game without opponent, even the rules are at hazard, and the players become emptiness and despair and all the riddles are blind. A voice will scream out, 'How long has it been?' And you'll wonder how long has it been since you've been home where no one lives anyway!

Derek I don't want to get caught in the middle. That's between you and Diego. It's nothing personal, George. Just business.

George Yeah. I understand. Just business. Right.

"Fuck you!"

Diego Oh, boo hoo, boo hoo.
So sad, George. I stole your California
connection. So what?
Who introduced you to Pablo Esobar?
Me!
Who introduced you to your fucking
Colombian wife?
Me!
Who protected you when my friend
Cesar Roza wanted to slice your
fucking throat out, huh?
Who made you millions and millions
of dollars?
Me!
And what do I get in return?
This?
Accusations?
I have always given you everything,
George, but that is over now. This is
my operation, my dream. So, go
home, George. Go back to your
stupid little life. You can sell half
grams to your fucking relatives for all
I care, because you are out!

"You'd better kill me now, Diego, because you're a dead man."

Revenge
George Jung

Tasting the sweet with the bitter, there is always the conscious self and how the self must preserve its integrity. How to pump up the ego in order to excel. To play the game of all games, you have to select yourself to be extraordinary in order to manufacture enough fuel to carry on. In order to play one must simply be in the right place at the right time, as the Gods so list. As if struck by a thunderbolt you suddenly become aware of your destiny. Tell all the truth but tell it with a slant.

The wave crashed on the beach at Norman's Cay with a man in the wind and the west moon. In a sense betrayal always lurked in the shadows. It is a fear only outlaws and lovers know. The way up and the way down are one and the same. It's been a long time since the cat-eyed, greedy son-of-a-bitch exposed himself with the same venom-tipped claws ripped into the soul and the truth's superb surprise. Tell all the truth but tell it with a slant.

You can walk away now that the cards of betrayal are cast upon the table. Leave, crumbling on the edge of the abyss, wondering forever how your vision became clouded, your faculties weakened, worn in body and soul and betrayed by simple-minded, common people. Leave now, no more the common passenger on the coach of destiny; no longer a giant of action, all the greatness of a star burned out locked only in obsession for revenge knowing how foolish serious people can become.

It was like falling down a deep black mine of shock, incomprehension and flailing depths of impossible revenge and hatred. I was a satyr with an arrow in his heart, killed by a beloved brother. It was all unforgivable and vile.

The mind now wondered into a bottomless madness and was swept away. A conspiracy beyond all the powers of love or hate, realizing for the very first time everything had been opposite with double meanings, double dialogue.

It was fucking inconceivable, equal in humiliation. I'd never been more lost or violent.

Why could I not see the transparently double-meaning dialogue? In all it was simple, he played. I know now that I was the judge only in name and that I was finally the judged to be judged by my own judgement. The marionette would make the manipulation of the strings wait! While the anger turned to sadness and on into mercilessness.

It was clear that the Gods don't exist to answer – we must answer the Gods!

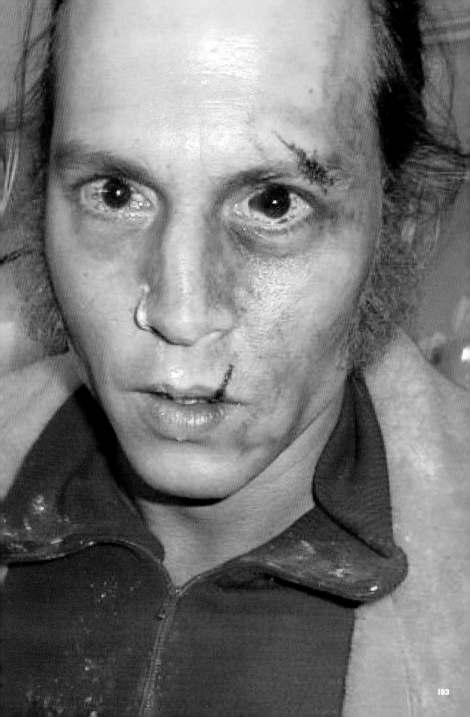

"Jesus Christ."

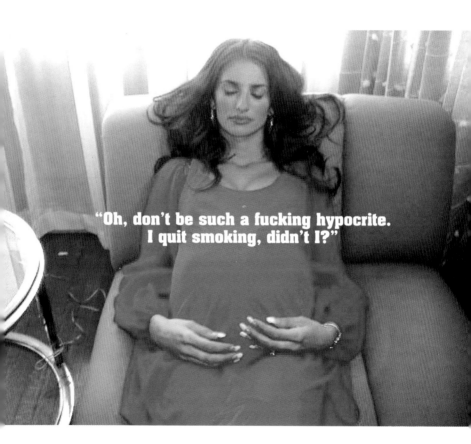

"Oh, don't be such a fucking hypocrite.
I quit smoking, didn't I?"

"Put that shit away."

"Oh, fucking relax.
Let your hair down for once.
It's your fucking birthday, for Chrissakes.
You're such a fucking pussy.

I swear to God, I married this big time drug
dealer and wound up with the maid."

"Happy birthday, George."
"Cops! They're all over the place."
"Freeze!"

Ermine Don't you dare step foot in this house. You're not my son, you hear me?

"I don't have a son anymore."

"He's a fugitive and a fucking cocaine dealer! There's a kilo in his trunk right now. Take this sorry motherfucker to jail."

"What's this?"

"It's a statement. How it was all yours, the pound of coke was for personal use and none of the guests had any idea it was there, yeah, right."

"I want my kid out of protective custody. Now. No fucking around. My wife and my kid on a plane tonight. I sign when they call me safe and sound."

Mirtha I'm divorcing you, George. I'm getting custody of Kristina.

"And when you get out next week, you're going to pay support, and that's the end of it. All right?"

There's someone else. I'm sorry.

You should've taken better care of me, you know? You've been away a long time. Four years. Say something.

George What do you want me to say? I'm in prison. You should know. You put me here.

Mirtha Fuck you, George. I knew you'd say something like that. Always thinking about yourself.

Kristina
EMMA ROBERTS

Loss of a child's faith
George Jung

An act of betrayal etched across a child's face will suffocate you. It's not negotiable and one realizes the beginning of the end. Life ceases to be fascinating and a conduit of emotions short out your heart. I had betrayed my daughter more than once. Looking down at her I began to deny it, but she turned and walked, leaving me in a pool of palpable sleaziness I'd not known before. I stood there trying to pull from airy nothings. It all ran – maybe I couldn't take care of her and never well intended to. Selfishness abounded. I couldn't live without her and there was the real question of whether I cared about living at all. Standing there with a chill in my head that made all questions and answers moot. There was no safe place to run. It was all painfully accurate; wanting to turn it off, but could not. I was mournfully going off the deep end knowing my child no longer cared. It was all for nought and worthless. The words echoed in my head, 'Die and fade away.' You know who I am, I never meant to treat you unkind. I have reasons but no time. A faith has been broken. I don't have much pride knowing I mortgaged my whole life and couldn't make the next payment. The sun exploded into a million pieces along with my heart, impossible to replace. It's damn well true a man can stand alone, but what is truly the self if others no longer stand by him? Are we not all woven into a delicate pattern of togetherness and love? It's dark and the wind screams all I am or ever will be…

George Hello, Derek?

It's George. Yeah.

Yeah, I am. I'm in Miami.

I'm looking to do something.
I want to put together a crew.

Do you know anybody?

Leon?

I don't know him.

What's his last name?

All right.

Give me the number.

"ARE WE GOOD?
YEAH, WE'RE
GOOD. WE'RE
BEAUTIFUL,
WE'RE
PERFECT. THIS
IS ONE

HUNDRED PERCENT PURE COLUMBIAN COCAINE, LADIES AND GENTLEMEN. DISCO SHIT...

"A man must look at his life and think it luxury."

Credits

Thanks

Photography Ted Demme

Design Nuisance

Managing Editor Zoe Manzi

Creative Director Kirk Teasdale

Production Steve Savigear and Emily Moore

'Blow by Blow' first published in Great Britain in 2001
by Vision On Publishing Ltd
112-116 Old Street
London EC1V 9BG
T +44 (0)20 7336 0766
F +44 (0)20 7336 0966
www.visiononpublishing.com
info@visiononpublishing.com

Ted Demme would like to thank: Amanda, Jaxon,
George Jung and family, Bob Friedman, Dave Imhoff,
Nick Cassavetes, David McKenna, Johnny Depp, Penelope
Cruz, Paul Reubens, Franka Potente, Rachel Griffiths, Ray
Liotta and the entire cast and crew of Blow; David A.
Stewart, Christi Dembrowski, Mike Scheer, Zoe Manzi, Kirk
Teasdale and everyone at Vision On Publishing, Tracy
Flaco, Jennifer Eatz, Lance Stockton and Eric Brown - and
a special thanks to Emma Tillinger.

Vision On would like to thank: Sarah Jane, Briar,
Diana, Sarah, Ed and Ronny at Vision On, Alex Proud,
Rankin, Diana Beer, Tracy McCrory and Tracy Lorie at New
Line and Daniel Shnider at United Talent.

 www.visiononpublishing.com